Step by Step Guide to the Driving Test Manoeuvres

Plus extra bonus of show me tell me questions

written by

Debbie Brewer

Also by Debbie Brewer

What to Expect on your Driving Test: A Complete Guide

Show Me Tell Me Questions for the Driving Test

Inspiration: Nuggets of Wisdom and Motivational Mantras

Poetry Treasures

Volume One

Volume Two

Volume Three

Volume Four

www.amazon.com/author/debbiebrewer

Contents

Foreword

Acknowledgements

The New Driving Test

Frequently Asked Questions

Test Manoeuvres

    Reverse Parallel Park

    Reverse Bay Park

    Forward Bay Park

    Right Reverse

Emergency Stop

Non-Test Manoeuvres

    Turn in the Road

    Left Corner reverse

Right Corner Reverse

Conclusion

Show me Tell me Questions

Connect with the Author

Foreword

Dear reader and future driver,

As a DVSA Approved Driving Instructor, I regularly teach manoeuvres to my pupils enabling them to become skilled at reversing and turning the car in various situations whilst keeping themselves and everyone around them safe and with minimal inconvenience to other road users.

While doing so, I have often been asked to write down simple sets of instructions in a step by step form to help them understand how to perform the manoeuvre.

Some find it helpful to take home and refer to when they are practicing in their own cars. Some find that just by re-reading how they did the manoeuvre in the lesson helps embed that new knowledge into their memories.

As a past Ordit registered Instructor Trainer, I have also been asked by other instructors, (PDIs and ADIs) how I teach manoeuvres to my pupils.

There are many different methods for teaching manoeuvres available, but those listed here are the ones that I have found most useful.

However you decide to use this guide, I hope its simple step by step approach, and its section on frequently asked questions help you to understand and improve, and enables you to perform manoeuvres more safely and skilfully in the future.

And finally, at the end of this book, I have added an extra handy bonus section, of all the up to date DVSA 'Show Me Tell Me' questions, for the pupil to refer to and revise.

Enjoy, and good luck with your future driving!

Acknowledgements

With thanks to my mother for passing on her writing flair,

my father for his great spelling, grammar and logic genes, and love of driving

my husband for his patience when I am in my writing zone,

and not forgetting my wonderful colleagues in the Driving Instructor community.

Dedicated to my children,

Ben and Samantha

The New Driving Test

On 4th December 2017, the UK driving test changed.

"The changes are designed to make sure new drivers have the skills they'll need to help them through a lifetime of safe driving." (DVSA 2017)

Basically, the DVSA believed that the old style driving test no longer tested pupils on the type of driving skills that they were more likely to be using in today's modern driving environment once they had passed their test.

The main changes involved:

> Changes to the type of manoeuvre you could be asked to do
>
> Changes in the show me tell me questions
>
> Use of satnav

Over the course of this book, I plan to describe, in easy to follow step by step stages, how to do each manoeuvre that you are required to know for your driving test. You will be asked to demonstrate one of these on the test. These are:

Reverse Parallel park

Reverse bay park

Forward bay park

Right reverse.

I will also explain the Emergency Stop, so that you can prepare and practice for your driving test. Only one in three tests will be asked to perform the emergency stop, but you will still have to do one manoeuvre as well.

Furthermore, I have included three extra manoeuvres that you might like to learn to improve your general driving skill, but which are no longer tested in the driving test. These are:

Turn in the road

Left corner reverse

Right corner reverse

Finally, I have added a bonus section with the most up to date DVSA Show Me Tell Me Questions that you will need to know for your driving test.

But first, let's have a look at some frequently asked questions that pupils often ask.

Frequently Asked Questions

What manoeuvres will I be tested on?

You will be asked to perform one of the following manoeuvres: Reverse Parallel Park, Reverse Bay Park, Forward Bay Park, Right Reverse.

Will I have to do an Emergency Stop?

One in three tests are asked to demonstrate the emergency stop. If you do have to do one, you will also have to do one manoeuvre. It does not replace the manoeuvre.

At what speed should I do my manoeuvres?

You will find that the slower you perform the manoeuvre, the easier it becomes, because you give yourself time to be more accurate with your thinking and steering. Remember the clutch control and speed you use when you are 'peeping and creeping' out of a closed junction? It is the same speed and same clutch control that you will use for your manoeuvre. Note, the examiner will not be timing you when you perform your manoeuvre on test.

What observations should I do?

Before and during your manoeuvre, you must continually do effective observations, looking all around the car for any hazards, which may include vehicles, motorcycles, bicycles, pedestrians, etc.

What should I do if another vehicle approaches while I am doing my manoeuvre?

When you are about to start your manoeuvre, imagine your car is in the centre of a bubble that stretches six car lengths away from your car and all around the car. When any moving hazard, i.e. vehicle, motorbike, bicycle, pedestrian, etc, enters the perimeter of that bubble, you should bring your car to a stop, until, either they continue out of the bubble, or they become stationary. Then you may continue your manoeuvre, ensuring the area remains safe by continual effective observations all around the car.

What is 'dry steering?'

Dry steering means turning the steering wheel without moving the car. You should try to avoid dry steering as it can damage your steering mechanism and your tyres.

What if I am doing a manoeuvre on a hill?

If you are moving downhill, you may find you have to put the clutch down and control the speed of the car using the brake.

What is 'full lock'?

Full lock means turning the steering wheel as far as it goes in any one direction.

When should I select reverse gear?

When you are getting ready to perform your manoeuvre, you should prepare the car in reverse gear as soon as you can, even if you are waiting for another moving hazard to pass, as this will put on your reverse lights at the back of your car, which is a signal to any hazards behind you that lets them know you are planning to reverse.

What is 'POM'?

POM is an acronym that stands for **P**repare, **O**bserve, **M**ove. It is the order in which you should start your manoeuvre to keep it safe. We will refer to the POM routine as we go on to discuss how to perform the manoeuvre.

What is the examiner looking for when I perform a manoeuvre on test?

The examiner will be looking to see if you are doing effective observations all around the car, if you are showing good clutch control by keeping the manoeuvre slow, and they will be looking for reasonable accuracy.

Will I have to complete my manoeuvre in one move?

No, you can adjust your position by doing a correction. You don't have to get it right first time. I have included step by step instructions on how to correct each manoeuvre in this book.

My car has cameras and parking sensors. Can I use these during my manoeuvre?

Yes, **but,** (and this is a big but), you must be doing effective observations all around the car as well. This is because the camera and sensors only tell you what is behind your car. But if a child runs from either side of the car, you need to see the child before he/she gets behind the car, so you can stop the vehicle in time.

Test Manoeuvres

You will be asked to demonstrate one of the following manoeuvres while on your driving test.

These are:

1. Reverse Parallel Park
2. Reverse Bay Park
3. Forward Bay Park
4. Right Reverse

Parallel Park

The reverse parallel park enables you to park the car next to the curb between cars. When you park your car in this manner, ensure you have chosen a safe, legal and convenient place, and leave enough room for any parked vehicles in front or behind to be able to easily manoeuvre out from their spaces.

On your driving test, you should complete this entire manoeuvre within a space of two car lengths. You should start this manoeuvre at the side of the road, at a distance of about one car length behind another parked car.

If you are performing this manoeuvre on a downhill gradient, you may have to put the clutch down and use the brake to control the speed.

To keep this manoeuvre safe, you must continue to make effective observations for hazards while you are moving.

Method for Reverse Parallel Park

Stage One:

Prepare:

Prepare the car in first gear.

Find the biting point with the clutch.

Observe for hazards:

Check the middle mirror.

Look all around the car.

Check right blind spot.

Move:

Release the handbrake.

Let the car start to creep.

Steer to the right.

Move the car forward, around the parked car and then steer to the left until you are next to the parked car. Make your steering straight so your wheels are straight.

You should have a distance of 1 metre (one car door length) between the side of your car and the parked car.

Continue creeping forward until you are halfway past the parked car.

Brake.

Stage Two:

Prepare:

Prepare the car in reverse gear.

Find the biting point with the clutch.

Observe for hazards:

Check the middle mirror.

Look all around the car.

Look over your left shoulder out of the back windscreen.

Move:

Release the brake.

Let the car creep straight back until it is halfway past the parked car.

Look over to your right blind spot. (This is because the front of the car is going to swing out as you continue this manoeuvre so you need to know that it is clear and safe).

Look back over your left shoulder out of the back window.

Apply full lock to the steering to the left.

Let the car creep round until you reach a 2 o'clock position.

Keep looking around the car for hazards.

Now apply full lock to the steering to the right.

Let the car creep back until it is straight behind the parked car.

Do not get too close to the curb. (If you are getting too close to the curb, stop and move to Stage 3A for a correction).

Make the steering straight so the wheels are straight.

Apply hand brake and select neutral.

Now ask yourself, have you positioned the car in a reasonable parked position within a drains width of the curb?

If yes, well done. You have completed the manoeuvre!

If no, then you need to do a correction. If you are too far away from the curb, move on to Stage 3B for a correction.

Corrections for the Reverse Parallel Park

Stage 3A: If you are too close to the curb:

Prepare:

Prepare the car in first gear.

Find the biting point with the clutch.

Observe for hazards:

Look all around the car.

Check right blind spot.

Move:

Release the brake.

Let the car creep forward.

Do half steer to the right.

When sufficiently away from the curb, straighten the steer.

Then do half steer to the left.

When the car is straight, straighten steer and brake to stop.

Prepare:

Prepare the car in reverse gear.

Find the biting point with the clutch.

Observe for hazards:

Look all around the car.

Look over the left shoulder out of the back windscreen.

Release the brake.

Let the car creep back until you are approximately one car length from the parked car.

Apply the handbrake and select neutral.

Now ask yourself, have you positioned the car in a reasonable parked position within a drains width of the curb?

If yes, well done. You have completed the manoeuvre!

If no, then you need to do another correction.

Stage 3B: If you are too far away from the curb:

Prepare:

Prepare the car in first gear.

Find the biting point with the clutch.

Observe for hazards:

Look all around the car.

Check right blind spot.

Move:

Release the brake.

Let the car creep forward.

Do half steer to the left.

When sufficiently close to the curb, straighten the steer.

Then do half steer to the right.

When car is straight, straighten steer and brake to stop.

Prepare:

Prepare the car in reverse gear.

Find biting point with the clutch.

Observe for hazards:

Look all around the car.

Look over left shoulder out of the back windscreen.

Move:

Release the brake.

Let the car creep back until you are approximately one car length from the parked car.

Apply handbrake and select neutral.

Now ask yourself, have you positioned the car in a reasonable parked position within a drains width of the curb?

If yes, well done. You have completed the manoeuvre!

If no, then you need to do another correction.

Reverse Bay Park

This manoeuvre is designed for you to safely demonstrate how you would reverse into a parking bay on the left or the right, correctly positioning all four wheels of the car within the lines of the parking bay.

If you are performing this manoeuvre on a downhill gradient, you may have to put the clutch down and use the brake to control the speed.

To keep this manoeuvre safe, you must continue to make effective observations for hazards while you are moving.

Method for Reverse Bay Park to the Left or the Right

Stage One:

Start with the car at a right angle (90') to a row of parking bays.

Prepare:

Prepare the car in reverse gear.

Find the biting point with the clutch.

Observe for hazards:

Check your right blind spot.

Look all around the car.

Look over your left shoulder out of the back windscreen.

Move:

Release the brake.

Let the car creep backwards.

When one of the lines that separate the bays lines up with the centre of the door, look around the car. (This is because the front of the car is going to swing out as you continue this manoeuvre so you need to know that it is clear and safe).

Apply full lock to the steering, in the direction of the bay you are turning into. Ie. If the bay is on the left, steer left. If it is on the right, steer right.

Let the car creep round into the bay.

When the car is straight, make the steering straight so the wheels are straight.

Let the car continue to creep straight back into the bay until the front of the car is behind the line.

Apply handbrake and select neutral.

Now ask yourself, are all four wheels in the parking bay?

If yes, well done, you have completed the manoeuvre!

If no, then you need to follow the next stage to do a correction.

Corrections for the Reverse Bay Park

Ask yourself, do you want the car to be more to the left (see stage 2A) or to the right (see stage 2B)

Stage 2A

If you want the car to be more to the left:

Prepare:

Prepare the car in first gear.

Find the biting point with the clutch.

Observe for hazards:

Look all around the car for any hazards.

Move:

Release the brake.

Let the car creep forward.

Put half steer to the left.

When the car has moved sufficiently to the left, straighten the steering.

Now do half steer to the right.

When the car is straight, steer straight so the wheels are straight.

Brake to stop.

If you have moved the car over enough, you should be able to see the lines either side of the bay you are aiming for in your door mirrors.

Prepare:

Now prepare the car in reverse gear.

Find the biting point with the clutch.

Observe for hazards:

Look all around the car.

Look over your left shoulder out of the back windscreen.

Move:

Release the brake.

Let the car creep straight back into the bay.

Stop when the front of the car is behind the line.

Apply handbrake and select neutral.

Now ask yourself, are all four wheels in the parking bay?

If yes, well done, you have completed the manoeuvre!

If no, then you need to do another correction. Refer back to Stage 2A or Stage 2B.

Stage 2B

If you want the car to be more to the right:

Prepare:

Prepare the car in first gear.

Find the biting point with the clutch.

Observe for hazards:

Look all around the car for any hazards.

Move:

Release the brake.

Let the car creep forward.

Put half steer to the right.

When car has moved sufficiently to the right, straighten the steering.

Now do half steer to the left.

When car is straight, steer straight so the wheels are straight.

Brake to stop.

If you have moved the car over enough, you should be able to see the lines either side of the bay you are aiming for in your door mirrors.

Prepare:

Now prepare the car in reverse gear.

Find the biting point with the clutch.

Observe for hazards:

Look all around the car.

Look over your left shoulder out of the back windscreen.

Move:

Release the brake.

Let the car creep straight back into the bay.

Stop when the front of the car is behind the line.

Apply handbrake and select neutral.

Now ask yourself, are all four wheels in the parking bay?

If yes, well done, you have completed the manoeuvre!

If no, then you need to do another correction. Refer back to Stage 2A or Stage 2B.

Forward Bay Park

This manoeuvre is designed for you to safely demonstrate how you would drive forward into a parking bay on the left or the right, correctly positioning all four wheels of the car within the lines of the parking bay.

If you are performing this manoeuvre on a downhill gradient, you may have to put the clutch down and use the brake to control the speed.

To keep this manoeuvre safe, you must continue to make effective observations for hazards while you are moving.

Method for Forward Bay Park to the Left or the Right

Stage One:

Start with the car at a right angle (90') to a row of parking bays.

Prepare:

Prepare the car in first gear.

Find the biting point with the clutch.

Observe for hazards:

Look all around the car.

Check your right blind spot.

Move:

Release the brake.

Let the car creep backwards.

If driving forward into a bay on the right:

When one of the lines that separate the bays lines up with the centre of the door, look around the car, (as you need to know that it is clear and safe).

Apply full lock to the steering, in the direction of the bay you are turning into, i.e. right.

If you are driving forward into a bay on the left:

If you are turning into a bay on the left, you may have to check your middle mirror, and then your right mirror to ensure no one is overtaking you, and then swing out to the right side of the road in order to get enough turn to get into the bay on the left.

When one of the lines that separate the bays lines up with the centre of the door, look around the car, (as you need to know that it is clear and safe).

Apply full lock to the steering, in the direction of the bay you are turning into, i.e. left.

Stage Two

Let the car creep round into the bay.

When the car is straight, make the steering straight so the wheels are straight.

Let the car continue to creep straight forward into the bay until the back of the car is behind the line.

Apply handbrake and select neutral.

Now ask yourself, are all four wheels in the parking bay?

If yes, well done, you have completed the manoeuvre!

If no, then you need to follow the next stage to do a correction.

Corrections for the Forward Bay Park

Ask yourself, do you want the car to be more to the left (see stage 3A) or to the right (see stage 3B)

Stage 3A

If you want the car to be more to the left:

Prepare:

Prepare the car in reverse gear.

Find the biting point with the clutch.

Observe for hazards:

Look all around the car for any hazards.

Look over your left shoulder out of the back windscreen

Move:

Release the brake.

Let the car creep backwards.

Put half steer to the left.

When the car has moved sufficiently to the left, straighten the steering.

Now do half steer to the right.

When the car is straight, steer straight so the wheels are straight.

Brake to stop.

If you have moved the car over enough, you should be able to see the lines either side of the bay you are aiming for in front of you.

Prepare:

Now prepare the car in first gear.

Find the biting point with the clutch.

Observe for hazards:

Look all around the car.

Move:

Release the brake.

Let the car creep straight forward into the bay.

Stop when the back of the car is behind the line.

Apply handbrake and select neutral.

Now ask yourself, are all four wheels in the parking bay?

If yes, well done, you have completed the manoeuvre!

If no, then you need to do another correction. Refer back to Stage 3A or Stage 3B.

Stage 3B

If you want the car to be more to the right:

Prepare:

Prepare the car in reverse gear.

Find the biting point with the clutch.

Observe for hazards:

Look all around the car for any hazards.

Look over your left shoulder out of the back windscreen.

Move:

Release the brake.

Let the car creep backwards.

Put half steer to the right.

When car has moved sufficiently to the right, straighten the steering.

Now do half steer to the left.

When car is straight, steer straight so the wheels are straight.

Brake to stop.

If you have moved the car over enough, you should be able to see the lines either side of the bay you are aiming for in front of you.

Prepare:

Now prepare the car in first gear.

Find the biting point with the clutch.

Observe for hazards:

Look all around the car.

Move:

Release the brake.

Let the car creep straight forward into the bay.

Stop when the back of the car is behind the line.

Apply handbrake and select neutral.

Now ask yourself, are all four wheels in the parking bay?

If yes, well done, you have completed the manoeuvre!

If no, then you need to do another correction. Refer back to Stage 3A or Stage 3B.

Right Reverse

This manoeuvre is designed for you to safely park on the right side of the road, facing the oncoming traffic, and demonstrate a safe straight line reverse.

If you are moving downhill, you may find you have to put the clutch down and control the speed of the car using the brakes.

To keep this manoeuvre safe, you must continue to make effective observations for hazards while you are moving.

Method for the Right Reverse

Stage One

Prepare:

Start driving on the left side of the road.

Slow and prepare the car in first gear.

Find the biting point with the clutch.

Observe for hazards:

Check middle mirror.

Check right mirror.

Move:

Check there is no oncoming traffic.

If safe, put your right signal on.

Move across the road.

Pull up on the right side of the road.

You should be a drains width away from the curb.

Stage Two

Hint: have a look over your left shoulder out of the back windscreen to see where the curb behind cuts into the car. This point is your straight line reference point.

Remembering this reference point will help you when you perform your manoeuvre as it shows you how close to the curb you should be.

Prepare:

Select reverse gear.

Find the biting point with the clutch.

Observe for hazards:

Look all around the car.

Look over your left shoulder out of the back windscreen.

Move:

Let the car start to creep.

Move the car straight back.

Keep looking from your left shoulder, around the car to your right shoulder and back.

Remember: you must continue to make effective observations for hazards while you are moving.

Continue to let the car creep back.

Now look for your straight line reference point and follow instruction **A** or instruction **B**.

A:

If the curb is left of the straight line reference point, then quarter steer to the left.

When straight line reference point lines up with the curb, then quarter steer to the right.

When car is straight, make steering straight so wheels are straight.

B:

If the curb is right of the straight line reference point, then quarter steer to the right.

When straight line reference point lines up with the curb, then quarter steer to the left.

When car is straight, make steering straight so wheels are straight.

After completing instruction A or B:

Continue reversing, keeping curb lined up with your straight line reference point until you have moved two car lengths back.

Brake to stop.

Apply handbrake and select neutral.

You should have finished within a drains width of the curb.

Well done, you have completed this manoeuvre!

Correction for Right Corner Reverse

If you are too close to the curb:

If at any time during this manoeuvre you find that you are too close to the curb, you must stop.

You should not hit the curb or you may damage your tyres and if you mount the curb you could be a threat to any pedestrians.

Prepare:

Prepare the car in first gear.

Find the biting point with the clutch.

Observe for hazards:

Look all around the car.

Check your right blind spot.

Move:

Let the car creep forward and do half steer to the left moving the car away from the curb.

When car has moved sufficiently away, straighten the wheels and then do half steer to the right.

When the car is straight, make the steering straight so the wheels are straight.

Now you may continue your reversing manoeuvre.

Prepare:

Prepare the car in reverse gear.

Find the biting point with the clutch.

Observe for hazards:

Look all around the car.

Look over left shoulder out of back windscreen.

Move:

Let the car creep back and continue the manoeuvre as per previous instructions, **A** or **B**.

Well done, you have completed the correction!

Emergency Stop

Whilst driving normally, you should be checking your middle mirror at least every five seconds. If you see a warning sign, or any potentially hazardous situation, you should check your middle mirror so that you know the true distance and speed of vehicles behind you. It may also be sensible to reduce your speed, especially if you see that a vehicle is too close behind you in this circumstance.

These actions will reduce your chances of needing to do an emergency stop and will give the vehicle behind you more time to react if you do have to stop suddenly.

When performing an emergency stop, you must react quickly.

You may find that if your wheels lock up under harsh braking, the anti-lock braking system (ABS) comes on if your car has this system. If it does come on you may feel the brake pedal juddering under your foot and the car may be making a loud low grinding noise. Do not worry... you have not broken anything! Just keep braking.

If your car does not have ABS, and the wheels lock up during harsh braking, then release and re-apply the brake pedal, and continue to do so until the wheels unlock. This is called cadence braking.

Very rarely, you may find the car will begin to skid. If the back of the car skids to the left, you should steer to the left, enabling the wheels to re-grip the road. Similarly, if the back of the car skids to the right, you should steer to the right, enabling the wheels to re-grip the road.

Method for the Emergency Stop

Stage One

You will be driving normally.

Now, imagine a child has run out in front of your car.

You should already have been checking your mirror at least every five seconds so you should already know what is behind you. You do not want to waste time checking your mirror now.

Keep looking ahead of you.

Keep your steering straight.

With quick reactions, press firmly down on your brake pedal.

Press your clutch to the floor.

Keep both feet down on both pedals until the car has come to a stop.

Apply the handbrake.

Select neutral.

Now you can relax your feet off the pedals.

Stage Two

Now imagine there will be a Mum and other people running towards the child to see if he is ok. They may be coming from any direction around your car.

Prepare:

Prepare the car in first gear.

Find the biting point with the clutch.

Observe for hazards:

You must look all around the car, from left to right, including blind spots, for any hazards. Remember, there might be a Mum and other people running towards the child to see if he is ok.

Move:

If it is safe, drive on.

Well done, you have completed this exercise!

Non-Test Manoeuvres

The following manoeuvres are not tested on the driving test, but nonetheless, are still useful to be able to do when you need to.

These are:

1. Turn in the Road
2. Left Corner Reverse
3. Right Corner Reverse

Turn in the Road

The turn in the road to face the other direction, is often mistakenly referred to as the three point turn. But you can perform this manoeuvre in as many turns as you need, depending on how narrow the road is. The more narrow the road, the more turns you will need to do to safely turn the car around without hitting the curb.

You may choose to do this manoeuvre if you find yourself at a dead end, or simply going the wrong way. Avoid doing this manoeuvre on a busy road, a one-way road, or a road with 'no u-turn' signs.

Hitting the curb should be avoided as you may damage your tyre, or you may mount the curb and pose a serious threat to a pedestrian.

When performing a turn in the road, you should try to stop at the end of each turn, so that your car does not overhang the curb. Again, if it does, you could pose a threat to a pedestrian.

Hint: When performing the turn in the road, if you creep very slowly and use big quick steering, you will get a tighter turn.

To keep this manoeuvre safe, you must continue to make effective observations for hazards while you are moving.

Method for the Turn in the Road

Stage One:

Prepare:

Start at the side of the road.

Prepare the car in first gear.

Find the biting point with the clutch.

Observe for hazards:

Check middle mirror.

Check left and right mirrors.

Look all around the car.

Check right blind spot.

Move:

Release the handbrake.

Let the car start to creep.

With big quick steers, put full lock on the steering to the right.

As you move over the centre of the road, you may find the camber of the road now slopes downhill, so you may have to put the clutch down and control the speed of the car at a creeping pace using the foot brake.

When the curb in front cuts in just under your right door mirror, brake to stop.

Stage Two:

Prepare:

Prepare the car in reverse gear.

Find the biting point with the clutch.

Observe for hazards:

Check the middle mirror.

Check over right shoulder.

Look all around the car.

Look over left shoulder out of back windscreen.

Move:

Release the brake.

Let the car start to creep.

With big quick steers, put full lock on the steering to the left.

When you reach the centre of the road, look all around the car.

Look over your right shoulder towards the curb behind.

Remember, the road might start to slope away, so you may have to put the clutch down and control the speed with the brake.

When the curb behind cuts into the bottom right corner of your right window, brake to stop.

Stage Three:

Prepare:

Prepare the car in first gear.

Find the biting point with the clutch.

Observe for hazards:

Look all around the car.

Have a last look left for any oncoming vehicles.

Look in the direction you will be going.

Move:

Release the brake.

Let the car start to creep.

With big quick steers, put full lock on the steering to the right.

Keep creeping forward making sure the front of the car clears the curb in front of you. (If it is not going to clear, brake to stop, and repeat stage two and three).

After clearing the curb in front, straighten the steering so the wheels are straight.

Check your middle mirror and right door mirror.

If safe, drive on.

Well done, you have completed this manoeuvre!

Left Corner Reverse

This manoeuvre is designed for you to safely change the direction you are travelling in if you find you are going the wrong way.

If you are moving downhill, you may find you have to put the clutch down and control the speed of the car using the brakes.

Before you do this manoeuvre, look closely at the curb you will be reversing round and ask yourself, how tight is the curve? Will it require half a steer, three quarter steer, or one full steer? The tighter the curve, the more steer it will require.

To keep this manoeuvre safe, you must continue to make effective observations for hazards while you are moving.

Method for the Left Corner Reverse

Stage One

Prepare:

Start on the left side of the road, with the road that you wish to reverse into in front of you.

Prepare the car in first gear.

Find the biting point with the clutch.

Observe for hazards:

Check middle mirror.

Look all around the car.

Check right blind spot.

Move:

Move away from the side of the road. Drive past the road you wish to reverse into.

As you drive past look into the road for any hazards such as parked cars, skips, children playing etc, which may mean you will have to find an alternative road to reverse into.

If the road you are driving past is clear, check middle mirror and left mirror.

If safe, pull up on the left, about two car lengths past the road and about a drains width from the curb.

A signal will only be required if it will benefit another road user.

Stage Two

Hint: Have a look over your left shoulder out of the back windscreen to see where the curb behind cuts into the car. This point is your straight line reference point.

Remembering this reference point will help you when you perform your manoeuvre as it shows you how close to the curb you should be.

Prepare:

Select reverse gear.

Find the biting point with the clutch.

Observe for hazards:

Look all around the car.

Look over your left shoulder out of the back windscreen.

Move:

Let the car start to creep.

Keep the car straight until the straight part of the curb of the new road you will be reversing into lines up with the bottom left corner of your back left window.

Now look over to your right blind spot. (This is because the front of the car is going to swing out as you continue this manoeuvre so you need to know that it is clear and safe).

Look around the car and back over your left shoulder out of the back window.

Now steer to the left. How much steer will depend on how tight the curve of the curb is. Will it require half a steer, three quarter steer, or one full steer? The tighter the curve, the more steer it will require.

Let the car creep around the curb into the new road.

When the car is straight in the new road, make the steering straight so the wheels are straight.

Remember: you must continue to make effective observations for hazards while you are moving.

Now look over your left shoulder out of the back windscreen.

Continue to let the car creep back.

Now look for your straight line reference point and follow instruction **A** or instruction **B**.

A:

If the curb is left of the straight line reference point, then quarter steer to the left.

When straight line reference point lines up with the curb, then quarter steer to the right.

When car is straight, make steering straight so wheels are straight.

B:

If the curb is right of the straight line reference point, then quarter steer to the right.

When straight line reference point lines up with the curb, then quarter steer to the left.

When car is straight, make steering straight so wheels are straight.

After completing instruction A or B:

Continue reversing, keeping curb lined up with your straight line reference point until you have moved three car lengths back from the give way line.

Brake to stop.

Apply handbrake and select neutral.

You should have finished within a drains width of the curb.

Well done, you have completed this manoeuvre!

Correction for Left Corner Reverse

If at any time during this manoeuvre you find that you are too close to the curb, you must stop.

You should not hit the curb or you may damage your tyres and if you mount the curb you could be a threat to any pedestrians.

Prepare:

Prepare the car in first gear.

Find the biting point with the clutch.

Observe for hazards:

Look all around the car.

Check your right blind spot.

Move:

Let the car creep forward and do half steer to the right moving the car away from the curb.

When car has moved sufficiently away, straighten the wheels and then do half steer to the left.

When the car is straight, make the steering straight so the wheels are straight.

Now you may continue your reversing manoeuvre.

Prepare:

Prepare the car in reverse gear.

Find the biting point with the clutch.

Observe for hazards:

Look all around the car.

Look over left shoulder out of back windscreen.

Move:

Let the car creep back and continue the manoeuvre as per previous instructions, **A** or **B**.

Well done, you have completed the correction!

Right Corner Reverse

This manoeuvre is designed for you to safely change the direction you are travelling in if you find you are going the wrong way.

If you are moving downhill, you may find you have to put the clutch down and control the speed of the car using the brakes.

Before you do this manoeuvre, look closely at the curb you will be reversing round and ask yourself, how tight is the curve? Will it require half a steer, three quarter steer, or one full steer? The tighter the curve, the more steer it will require.

To keep this manoeuvre safe, you must continue to make effective observations for hazards while you are moving.

Method for the Right Corner Reverse

Stage One

Prepare:

Start on the left side of the road, with the road that you wish to reverse into in front of you on the right.

Prepare the car in first gear.

Find the biting point with the clutch.

Observe for hazards:

Check middle mirror.

Look all around the car.

Check right blind spot.

Move:

Move away from the side of the road.

Check your middle mirror.

Check your right door mirror.

If safe, when you are halfway past the road on your right, put your right signal on.

Move across the road.

As you drive past, look into the road on the right for any hazards such as parked cars, skips, children playing etc, which may mean you will have to find an alternative road to reverse into.

Pull up on the right side of your road, about two car lengths past the road on the right.

You should be a drains width away from the curb.

Stage Two

Hint: have a look over your left shoulder out of the back windscreen to see where the curb behind cuts into the car. This point is your straight line reference point.

Remembering this reference point will help you when you perform your manoeuvre as it shows you how close to the curb you should be.

Prepare:

Select reverse gear.

Find the biting point with the clutch.

Observe for hazards:

Look all around the car.

Look over your left shoulder out of the back windscreen.

Move:

Let the car start to creep.

Move the car straight back.

Keep looking from your left shoulder, around the car to your right shoulder and back.

When curb on right starts to drop away from the back right wheel of the car, steer to the right.

How much steer will depend on how tight the curve of the curb is. Will it require half a steer, three quarter steer, or one full steer?

The tighter the curve, the more steer it will require.

Let the car creep around the curb into the new road.

When the car is straight in the new road, make the steering straight so the wheels are straight.

Remember: you must continue to make effective observations for hazards while you are moving.

Now look over your left shoulder out of the back windscreen.

Continue to let the car creep back.

Now look for your straight line reference point and follow instruction **A** or instruction **B**.

A:

If the curb is left of the straight line reference point, then quarter steer to the left.

When straight line reference point lines up with the curb, then quarter steer to the right.

When car is straight, make steering straight so wheels are straight.

B:

If the curb is right of the straight line reference point, then quarter steer to the right.

When straight line reference point lines up with the curb, then quarter steer to the left.

When car is straight, make steering straight so wheels are straight.

After completing instruction A or B:

Continue reversing, keeping curb lined up with your straight line reference point until you have moved five car lengths back from the give way line.

Brake to stop.

Apply handbrake and select neutral.

You should have finished within a drains width of the curb.

Well done, you have completed this manoeuvre!

Correction for Right Corner Reverse

If at any time during this manoeuvre you find that you are too close to the curb, you must stop.

You should not hit the curb or you may damage your tyres and if you mount the curb you could be a threat to any pedestrians.

Prepare:

Prepare the car in first gear.

Find the biting point with the clutch.

Observe for hazards:

Look all around the car.

Check your right blind spot.

Move:

Let the car creep forward and do half steer to the left moving the car away from the curb.

When car has moved sufficiently away, straighten the wheels and then do half steer to the right.

When the car is straight, make the steering straight so the wheels are straight.

Now you may continue your reversing manoeuvre.

Prepare:

Prepare the car in reverse gear.

Find the biting point with the clutch.

Observe for hazards:

Look all around the car.

Look over left shoulder out of back windscreen.

Move:

Let the car creep back and continue the manoeuvre as per previous instructions, **A** or **B**.

Well done, you have completed the correction!

Conclusion

I hope you have been able to use this guide to enhance your control, observation and accuracy while performing your manoeuvres. I have aimed to deconstruct each manoeuvre into simple sets of step by step instructions in order to maximise understanding.

I also hope that when you have passed your driving test and are driving independently, you will continue to apply the information in this guide to keep yourself and other road users safe.

My final two pieces of advice will be those that have correctly and continually re-occurred throughout this guide:

   1. **While performing any manoeuvre, you must**

continue to make effective observations for hazards both before and while you are moving.

2. The slower you perform the manoeuvre, the easier it becomes, as you give yourself time to be more accurate with your thinking and steering.

3.

    So go slow

And look everywhere!

Bonus Section
Show me Tell Me Questions

The examiner will ask you two questions:

- One 'tell me' question (where you explain how you'd carry out a safety task) at the start of your test, before you start driving.
-
- And one 'show me' question (where you show how you'd carry out a safety task) while you're driving.

'Show me' questions

1. When it's safe to do so, can you show me how you wash and clean the rear windscreen?

2. When it's safe to do so, can you show me how you wash and clean the front windscreen?

3. When it's safe to do so, can you show me how you'd switch on your dipped headlights?

4. When it's safe to do so, can you show me how you'd set the rear demister?

5. When it's safe to do so, can you show me how you'd operate the horn?

6. When it's safe to do so, can you show me how you'd demist the front windscreen?

7. When it's safe to do so, can you show me how you'd open and close the side window?

'Tell me' questions

1. Tell me how you'd check that the brakes are working before starting a journey.
Brakes should not feel spongy or slack. Brakes should be tested as you set off. Vehicle should not pull to one side.

2. Tell me where you'd find the information for the recommended tyre pressures for this car and how tyre pressures should be checked.
Manufacturer's guide, use a reliable pressure gauge, check and adjust pressures when tyres are cold, don't forget spare tyre, remember to refit valve caps.

3. Tell me how you make sure your head restraint is correctly adjusted so it provides the best protection in the event of a crash.
The head restraint should be adjusted so the rigid part of the head restraint is at least as high as the eye or top of the ears, and as close to the back of the head as is comfortable. Note: Some restraints might not be adjustable.

4. Tell me how you'd check the tyres to ensure that they have sufficient tread depth and that their general condition is safe to use on the road.

No cuts and bulges, 1.6mm of tread depth across the central three-quarters of the breadth of the tyre, and around the entire outer circumference of the tyre.

5. Tell me how you'd check that the headlights and tail lights are working. You don't need to exit the vehicle.
Explain you'd operate the switch (turn on ignition if necessary), then walk round vehicle (as this is a 'tell me' question, you don't need to physically check the lights).

6. Tell me how you'd know if there was a problem with your anti-lock braking system.
Warning light should illuminate if there is a fault with the anti-lock braking system.

7. Tell me how you'd check the direction indicators are working. You don't need to exit the vehicle.
Explain you'd operate the switch (turn on ignition if necessary), and then walk round vehicle (as this is a 'tell me' question, you don't need to physically check the lights).

8. Tell me how you'd check the brake lights are working on this car.
Explain you'd operate the brake pedal, make use of reflections in windows or doors, or ask someone to help.

9. Tell me how you'd check the power-assisted steering is working before starting a journey.

If the steering becomes heavy, the system may not be working properly. Before starting a journey, 2 simple checks can be made.

Gentle pressure on the steering wheel, maintained while the engine is started, should result in a slight but noticeable movement as the system begins to operate. Alternatively turning the steering wheel just after moving off will give an immediate indication that the power assistance is functioning.

10. Tell me how you'd switch on the rear fog light(s) and explain when you'd use it/them. You don't need to exit the vehicle.
Operate switch (turn on dipped headlights and ignition if necessary). Check warning light is on. Explain use.

11. Tell me how you switch your headlight from dipped to main beam and explain how you'd know the main beam is on.
Operate switch (with ignition or engine on if necessary), check with main beam warning light.

12. Open the bonnet and tell me how you'd check that the engine has sufficient oil.
Identify dipstick/oil level indicator, describe check of oil level against the minimum and maximum markers.

13. Open the bonnet and tell me how you'd check that the engine has sufficient engine coolant.
Identify high and low level markings on header tank where fitted or radiator filler cap, and describe how to top up to correct level.

14. Open the bonnet and tell me how you'd check that you have a safe level of hydraulic brake fluid.
Identify reservoir, check level against high and low markings.

Connect with the author

https://www.youtube.com/channel/UC1TTxfFTegJRN7fqNxkXmGg?app=desktop

www.amazon.com/author/debbiebrewer

https://www.clubdrive.co.uk/

https://www.facebook.com/DebbieBrewerPoetry

www.instagram.com/poetrytreasures

www.twitter.com/poetrytreasure